Scott Foresman
Reading

Take Me There

About the Cover Artist
Maryjane Begin and her family live in Providence, Rhode Island, where she teaches college
students when she is not working on her own art. Many of her illustrations—even of imaginary
places—show how things in Providence look.

ISBN 0-673-62157-X

4 5 6 7 8 9 10-VH-06 05 04 03 02 01 00

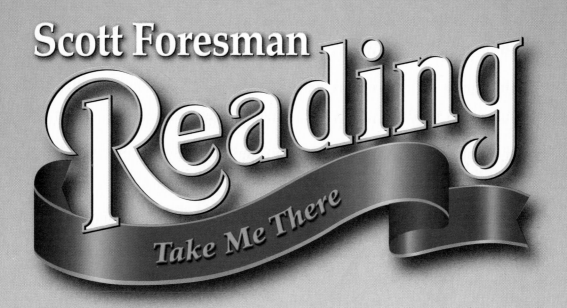

Scott Foresman Reading

Take Me There

Program Authors

Peter Afflerbach

James Beers

Camille Blachowicz

Candy Dawson Boyd

Deborah Diffily

Dolores Gaunty-Porter

Violet Harris

Donald Leu

Susan McClanahan

Dianne Monson

Bertha Pérez

Sam Sebesta

Karen Kring Wixson

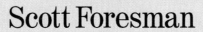

Scott Foresman

Editorial Offices: Glenview, Illinois • New York, New York
Sales Offices: Reading, Massachusetts • Duluth, Georgia • Glenview, Illinois
Carrollton, Texas • Menlo Park, California

Take Me There

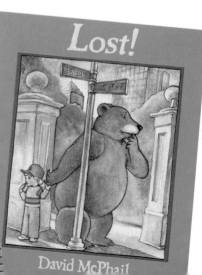

4

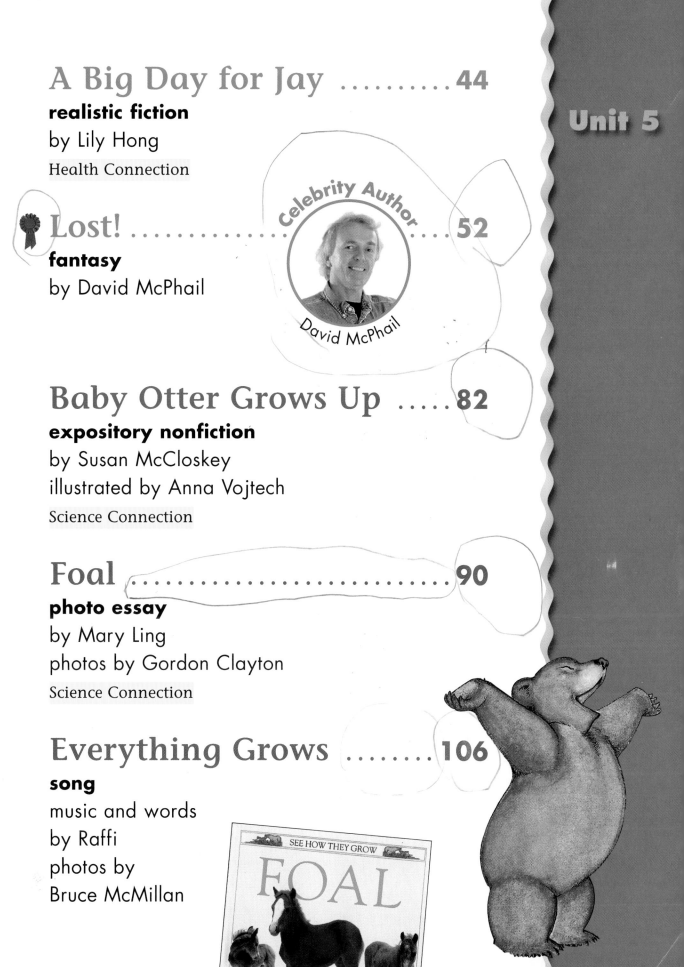

Unit 5

SEE HOW THEY GROW

FOAL

Take Me There

Where will we go?

How will we grow?

A Real Gift

by Diane Hoyt-Goldsmith

photos by
Lawrence Migdale

This is Nayeli Lopez.

She reads with her cat. She
gives him something to eat too.

Nayeli lives in the country.

She rides the bus to school.

It is loud, but Nayeli does not mind.

For Nayeli, loud sounds are soft.

It's hard for her to tell what people
are saying.

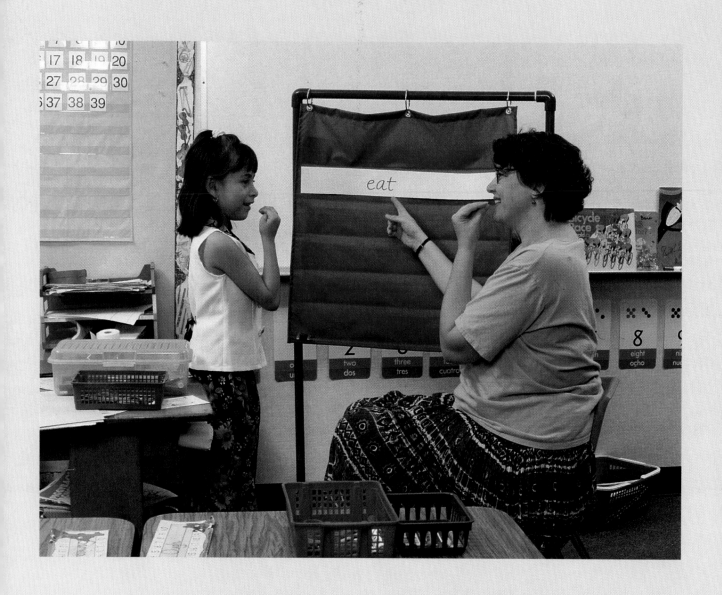

Nayeli can speak with her hands.
She knows how to make signs
for words.

One day, Nayeli had something to do. She met her mother right after school. "We can go now," her mother signed with her hands.

They stopped to buy a treat.

Nayeli picked out a peach to eat.

Then they passed a soccer team.

They stopped to watch the game.

Nayeli wanted to stay,

but she had something to do.

Nayeli saw a dog.

It wanted to play or be petted.

"No," signed her mother.

"I think we have to go now."

Nayeli walked very fast.

They had only one more block to go.

She didn't want to be late.

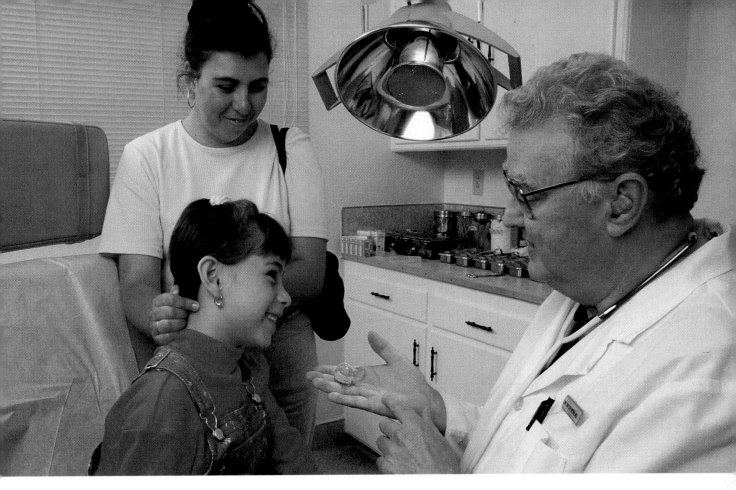

Now Nayeli had something to
help her. It fit just right.
The doctor's words sounded loud.

"Thank you" signed Nayeli
with her hands.

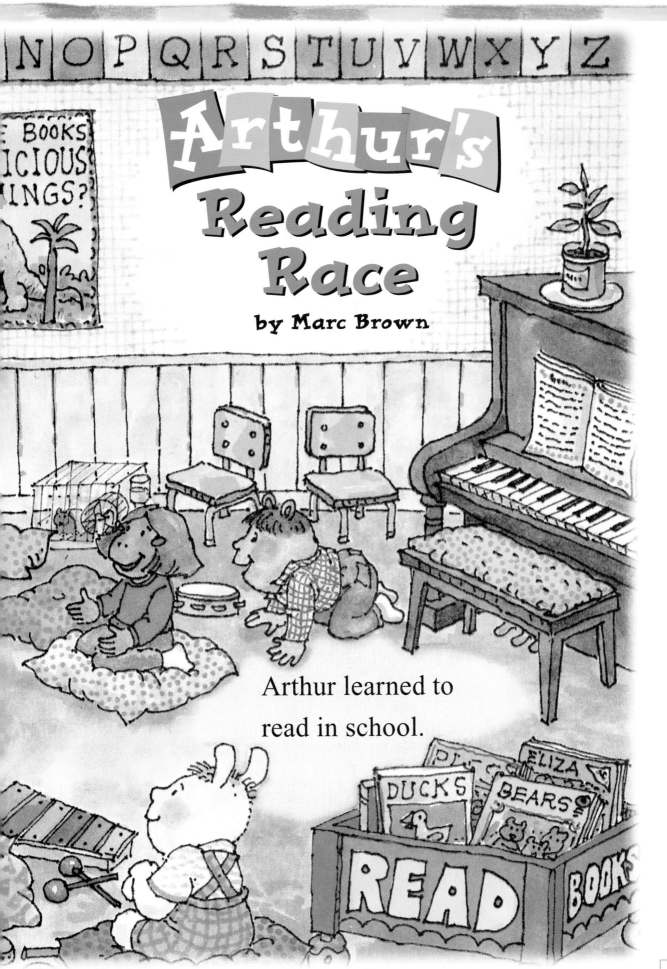

Arthur's Reading Race

by Marc Brown

Arthur learned to read in school.

Now Arthur reads everywhere!
He reads in the car.

He reads in bed.

He reads
to his puppy, Pal.

Arthur even reads
to his little sister, D.W.

One day Arthur said,
"I can teach YOU to read too."

"I already know how to read,"
said D.W.

"You do not!" said Arthur.

"Do too!" said D.W.

"Prove it," said Arthur.
"Read ten words, D.W.,
    and I'll buy you an ice cream."

D.W. stuck out her hand.
"It's a deal," she said.
"Let's go!"

They raced to the park.
Arthur pointed to a sign.
"What's that say?" he asked.

"Zoo," said D.W.
"Easy as pie."

"I spy three words,"
said Arthur.

"Me too," said D.W.

"Taxi, gas, milk."

Arthur stepped off the curb.

"Look out!" said D.W.
"It says Don't Walk.
You could get hit by a car."

"All right,
Miss Smarty-Pants,
what's that say?"
asked Arthur.

"Police," said D.W.
"And you better
keep off the grass
or the police will get you."

"Bank," said D.W.

"I have a bank.

I hide my money in it
so you can't find it.
Bank makes eight words."

"We're almost home,"
said Arthur.
"Too bad.
You only read
eight words.
No ice cream
for you today."

"Hold your horses," said D.W.
"I spy . . . ice cream.
Hot dog! I read ten words.
Let's eat!"

pizza chip   shoe lace

Bumpy road   moose ripple

frog chip

egg shell

D.W. and Arthur ran
to the ice cream store.
Arthur bought two big cones.

Strawberry for D.W.
and chocolate for himself.
"Yummy," said D.W.

Arthur sat down.

"Sit down with me," said Arthur,

"and I'll read you my book."

"No," said D.W.

"I'll read YOU the book."

Arthur shook his head.
"I don't think so," he said.
"There are too many words
that you don't know."

D.W. laughed.
"Get up, Arthur."

"Now I can teach you
    two words that you don't know,"
    said D.W.
"WET PAINT!"

About the Author and Illustrator

Marc Brown

Arthur is a very famous aardvark! Arthur first appeared years ago. Marc Brown's son wanted to hear a bedtime story. Mr. Brown told one about an aardvark. Now there are more than thirty books about Arthur and D.W. You may have even seen Arthur on TV.

Let's Talk

Find all the words D.W. read in the pictures. What other words can you find?

I Spy

1. Say, "I spy a word."
2. Give clues about the word.
3. Ask your friend to guess the word.

I spy a word. It is something red and juicy.

apple   bee   corn

It's the Best!

An **adjective** is a word that describes.

An adjective tells more about a person, place, or thing.

My **favorite** TV show is *Arthur.*

Arthur has a **little** sister named D.W.

They live in a **pretty** town.

Talk

Describe your favorite TV show.

Use adjectives.

Write

Write about a movie or TV show.

What adjectives describe it?

A Big Day for Jay

by Lily Hong

It was noisy and crowded. Jay tugged at his dad. "When can we ride the Fire Dragon?" asked Jay. "I can't wait and I'm not afraid." His dad didn't hear him.

He tugged at his mom. "This isn't fun, Mom. All the jars look the same. Don't you want to see the Fire Dragon?"

All she said was, "Okay, we'll go soon."

They walked by the animals.

"Pig," said little Kate.
"Cow," said Mother.
"Sheep," said Father.
"Fire Dragon!" yelled Jay as he read the sign.

They walked
from the tent to
the Fire Dragon.
People were
everywhere.
They were
going this way
and that. A girl
with a big gray dog
bumped into Jay.

"Mom, Dad," said Jay. No one called back. Jay knew where he was. But where was his family?

Then Jay spotted a police officer. He acted brave. "I'll be okay," he said. "I'll tell her my name and where I live."

"Let's go to the Lost and Found," said the police officer. "It's by the train. We can wait for your family there. Okay?"

"Did you get lost today too?" Jay asked the little pup at the Lost and Found.

Then the door opened.
"Dog!" said Kate.
"Jay!" said Mother.
"Now let's find the Fire Dragon!" smiled Father.

52

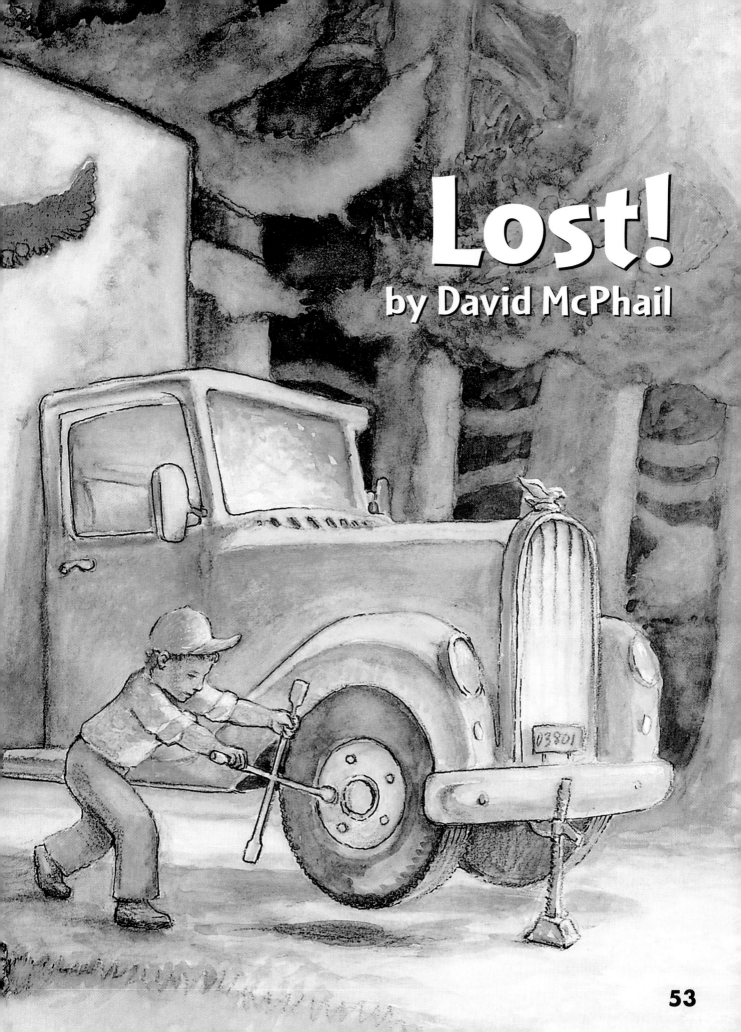

Lost!
by David McPhail

I am walking down the street
when I hear someone crying.

It's a bear!

He looks lost and afraid.

The tall buildings scare him.

And he's never seen so many people.

"Don't worry," I tell him.

"The buildings won't hurt you,
   and most of the people are friendly."

"How did you get here?" I ask.

"I climbed in to have a nap," he explains, "and when I woke up, I was *lost!*"

"I'll help you. Tell me where you live."

"There are trees where I live,"

he tells me.

So we find some trees.

"More trees," he says, "and water!"

I take him to a place where there
are more trees—and water too.
"No," he says. "This is not it either."

I have an idea. "Follow me!" I say.

I take him to a tall building.

We go inside, get on the elevator,
and ride all the way to the top.

From up here we can see the
whole city. "Look!" I say.
"Now we can find your home."

"There it is!" he says, pointing.

Down we go, across three
streets and into the park.

The park is not the bear's home
after all—but he likes it there.

We go for a boat ride,

we have lunch,

and we go to the playground.

We are having a good time.
But it is getting late, and the
bear is still lost.

"Let's try the library," I tell him.

"We can find out anything here!"

Inside the library we look
through lots of books.
The bear sees a picture that
looks like his home.

We find the place on a map and
hurry outside.

A bus is leaving.

We get on the bus and
ride for a long time.

Finally, we are there.

"*This* is where I live!" says

the bear.

He gives me a hug and
thanks me again for my help.
Then he waves good-bye and
disappears into the forest.

The trees are so tall, and
there aren't any people.
"Wait!" I call to the bear,
"come back!"

"I think I'm lost!" I tell him.

"Don't worry," he says.

"I will help you."

About the Author and Illustrator

David McPhail spends more time doing his artwork than he does writing his stories. When he gets an idea for a story, Mr. McPhail says, "It feels as if I'm about to win something." Do you feel that way about good ideas too?

Reader Response

Let's Talk

Would you help the bear?
Why or why not?

Write a Note

Write a note to the bear.
Tell him what he should do
if he gets lost again.

80

What Did You See?

Adjectives are words that describe.

Some adjectives tell about color.

Some adjectives tell about shape.

The boy met a **brown** bear.

They stopped to look at a **round** globe.

Talk

Tell about something you saw on your way to school. What color was it? What shape was it?

Write

Write a news story about your school. Use adjectives in your sentences.

Room 103 News

A Lost Bear
Today I was walking to school.
I saw a brown bear.
He was lost.

81

Baby Otter Grows Up

by Susan McCloskey
illustrated by Anna Vojtech

This is a baby otter. A baby
otter is called a kit. This kit is three
months old and still growing.

The kit rides on his mom's back.
He is holding on to her coat to keep
from slipping.

One day, his mom slips into the
water. This is something new!
   The kit is afraid. But his mom does
not go back to the land. She keeps
swimming around in the water.

Soon the kit's mom comes out
of the water. Then she slides in
again. This time, her kit likes
sailing on her back. Mom is like
a small boat.

One day the kit's mom swims
into deep water. The little kit is
holding on to her back. He seems
to like floating around.

Look! The kit's mom is sinking!
What will happen to the kit? Will
he sink or float?

The kit will float. He can swim!
But his mom had to show him that
he could.

Now the kit is almost grown. He
swims well. He swims around the
slow ducks. He can float on his
back too.

Best of all, he can play in the
water with his friends.

FOAL

by Mary Ling
photos by Gordon Clayton

Newborn

I am a foal, a newborn
pony. My legs are
very wobbly.

My mother feeds me her warm
milk as soon as I struggle to my feet.

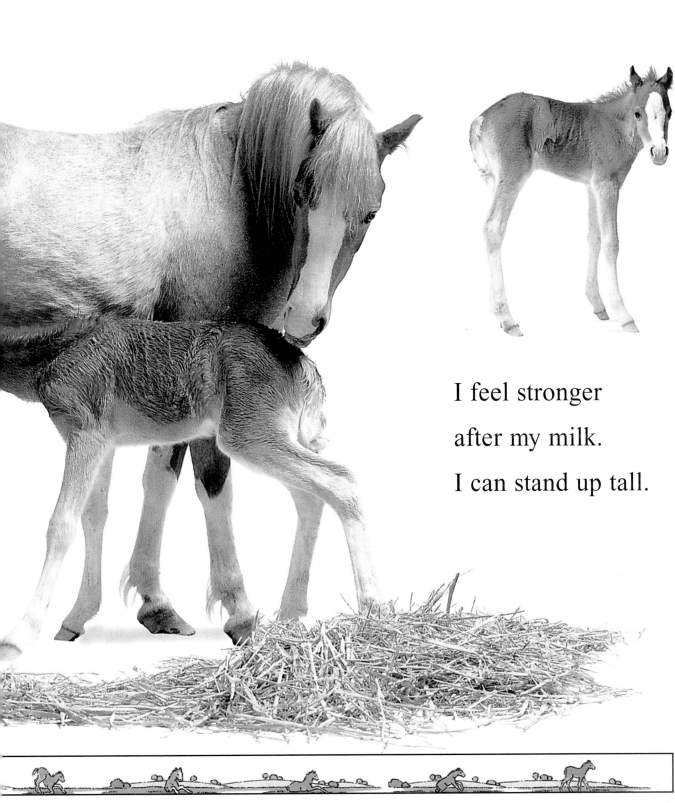

I feel stronger
after my milk.
I can stand up tall.

In the meadow

I am one week old.

I grow bigger every day.

I spend my days
in the meadow
with my mother.

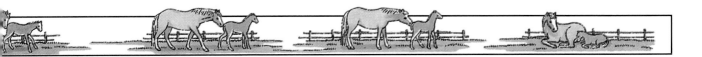

I cuddle close
to her when the
wind blows.

I love feeling
the soft grass
beneath my
hooves.

Looking for Mommy

I am two weeks old.

I have two new teeth.

I want to show my mother.

Where is she?

I neigh loudly to her.

I hope she hears me.

Soon my mother comes. She is never very far away.

Come and play

I am five weeks old.

Today will be a fun day!

A friend has come to play.

We play our
games and run
around the field.

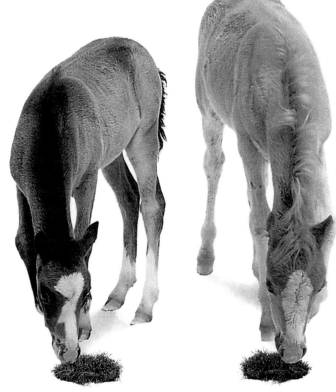

When we are
tired, we graze
together.
The fresh grass
tastes sweet.

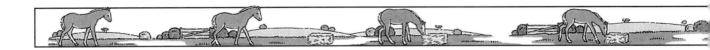

Crunchy apples

I am eight weeks old.
I gallop around the
fields every day.

Running and jumping
makes me very hungry.

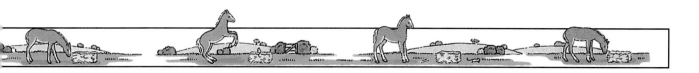

Look at these crunchy
red apples. They smell
yummy. I wonder if
I can eat one?

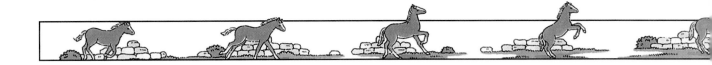

Long legs

I am four months old.

My coat is chestnut brown now.

My long legs are sturdy.

I do not wobble anymore.

I am growing taller every day.

I am almost as tall as my mother.

In the field

I am five months old and
nearly full-grown.

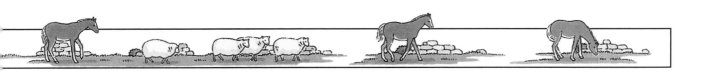

Soon I will be
big enough to
join the other
ponies in the field.

See how I grew

Newborn

One week old

Two weeks old

Five weeks old

Eight weeks old

Four months old   Five months old

Everything Grows

by Raffi

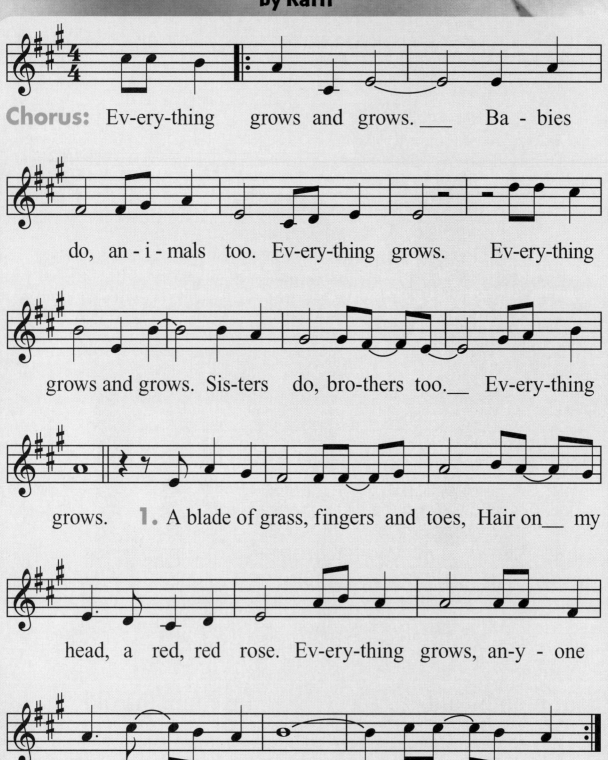

Chorus: Ev-ery-thing grows and grows. ___ Ba - bies do, an - i - mals too. Ev-ery-thing grows. Ev-ery-thing grows and grows. Sis-ters do, bro-thers too.__ Ev-ery-thing grows. **1.** A blade of grass, fingers and toes, Hair on__ my head, a red, red rose. Ev-ery-thing grows, an-y - one knows that's how it goes._____ Yes, ev - ery - thing

2. Food on the farm, fish in the sea,
   Birds in the air, leaves on the tree.
   Everything grows, anyone knows,
   That's how it goes.

3. That's how it goes, under the sun.
   That's how it goes, under the rain.
   Everything grows, anyone knows.
   That's how it goes.

Let's Talk

What ages did you enjoy reading about the most? Why?

Make an Album

What you need:

paper

pencils, crayons, or markers

What you do:

Work with a group.

Pick an animal.

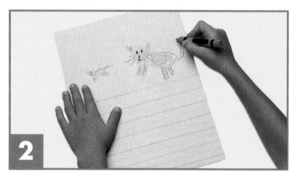

Draw the animal at more than one age.

Write what the animal can do.

Put your work in a class album.

Tiny Mice

Adjectives are words that describe. Some adjectives tell what size.

Baby Mice

Newborn mice are tiny. I have two big mice and six little babies. The babies have short tails and very small eyes.

Talk

Tell about something that grows. Use adjectives that tell about its size.

Write

Write a sentence like the first one in "Baby Mice." Will you use an adjective in your sentence?

What a Sight!

by Carolyn Crimi

illustrated by
Darryl Ligasan

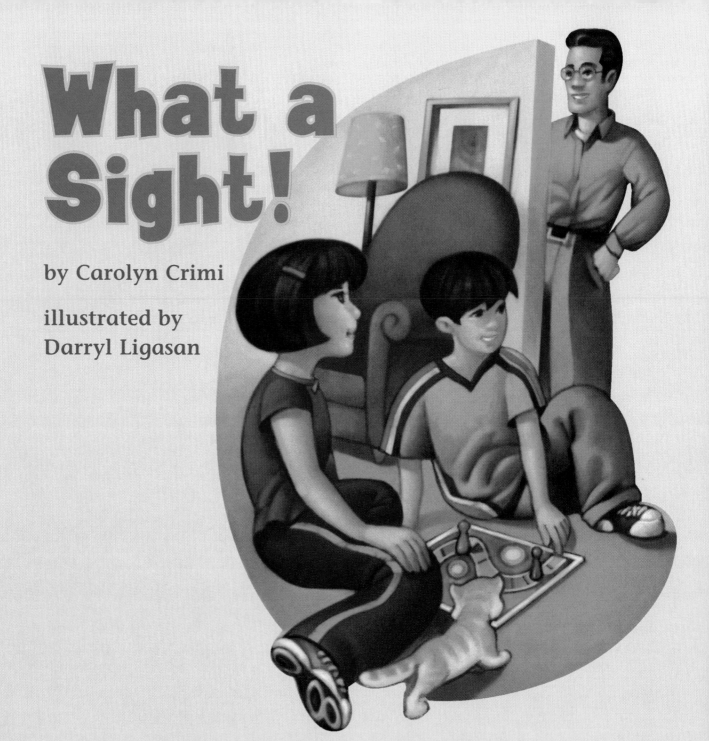

Nicky and Jim were playing together
with Nicky's game.
"We're going to the museum!"
Dad said.
"Right now?" asked Jim.
"I'll tell Mom first," said Dad.

Nicky petted Tiger's fur and sighed. "I wish we could bring Tiger. He might like to go. But I guess museums are not for cats."

"I think you're right," said Jim.

Jim and Nicky got dressed to go to the museum. They didn't see Tiger sneak into Jim's backpack. Tiger hid right inside.

Dad, Nicky, and Jim walked
down the museum's halls. They
looked at the bright paintings
hanging high on the walls. Tiger
looked out of Jim's backpack.

They saw an apple pie and a lion
that liked to lie in the shade. Tiger
seemed to like the lion the best.

Then Tiger saw a painting of a very big dog. It made him start to move around. He jumped out of Jim's backpack!

"Tiger!" Nicky called. "Is that you?"

Together, Nicky and Jim ran after Tiger. He gave one man a fright. Soon everyone ran after Tiger. What a sight! Jim found him at last.

Dad's face was red from running. "Tiger, it isn't right to sneak into a museum," he said.

"You've been a bad kitty," said Jim. "But I bet you had fun!"

Lost in the Museum

by Miriam Cohen

illustrated by
Lillian Hoban

"This is a big place,"
the teacher told the first grade.

"But if we all stay together,
nobody will get lost in the museum."

Danny said to Jim,
"I know where the dinosaur is.
Come on, I'll show you!"

Jim had never seen a dinosaur.
He ran after Danny.
And Willy and Sammy,
Paul, and George did too.

Anna Maria and Sara started after them.
"Come back! You'll get lost!" they called.

Danny slid down the hall very fast.
He slid into a room at the end.
Willy and Sammy, Paul, George, Jim,
Anna Maria, and Sara ran after him.

But Jim stopped.
He put his head way back.
He looked up.

Jim heard Willy say,
"That is some big chicken!"

"It's the dinosaur!" shouted Danny.

Jim came around the corner.
The dinosaur had his arms up over
Jim's head. The dinosaur's teeth
were smiling a fierce smile.

Paul said, "Look out, Jim!
He's going to get you!"

Jim turned and ran as fast as he could.
"Jim, stop! I was only fooling," Paul called.

The kids came running after Jim.
"Don't worry. He won't hurt you," said Sammy.

"That's right," Willy told Jim.
"They don't have dinosaurs anymore."

Paul put his arm around Jim.
Anna Maria said, "It's silly to be scared."
Jim knew it was silly.
He wished he could be brave.

"Come on, let's find the others," George said.

"I think we are lost," said Sara.

"I know where to go," Danny said.

They all hurried after him down the big
hall. But there were too many rooms.

"You got us lost," Anna Maria said
to Danny.

"My toe hurts," said George.

"Maybe we will have to stay here
all night," Paul said.

Jim thought about staying all night
with the dinosaur.
"I will go find the teacher," he said.
"You stay here in case she comes."

Jim went into many rooms. He kept
his eyes shut a little. If he saw the
dinosaur, he could shut them tight.

A big boy was looking at birds' eggs.
Jim said, "Have you seen my teacher?"
Before the big boy could answer,
Jim saw a red coat way down the hall.

Margaret had a red coat! Jim ran to see.
But somebody else was wearing
Margaret's coat!

Jim was so tired.
He had to find the teacher!
He had to bring her back to the kids!
He ran on.

Jim saw penguins playing in the snow like first graders. He saw a mother, father, and a child deer. The father stood with one foot in the air.

Jim stopped to rest.
The room was dark.
At first he couldn't see.

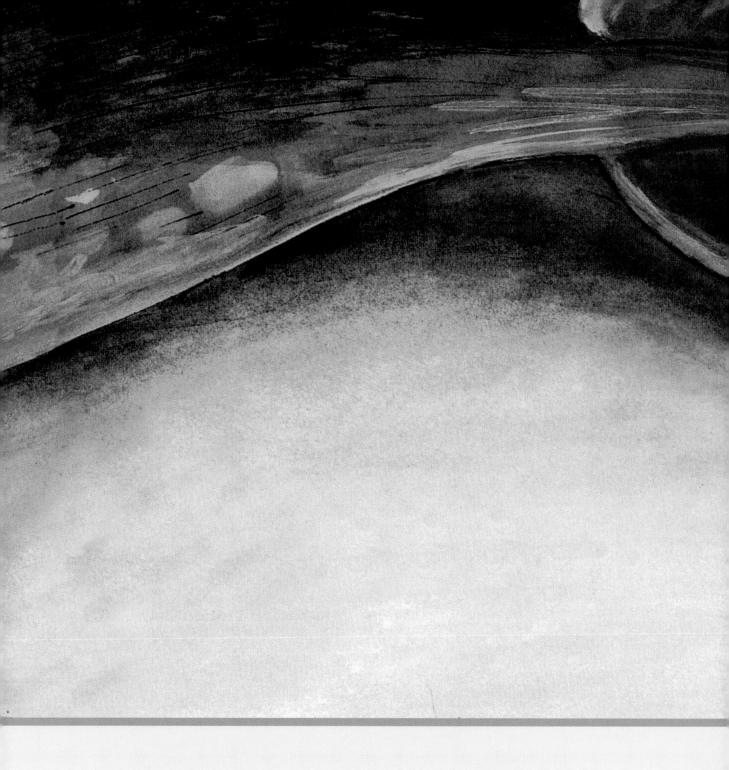

Then a great gray whale swam over
his head. He winked at Jim as if
he had something nice to tell him.
Jim looked all the way to the whale's tail.

A lady was there with many children.
"Jim!" everybody called. "Oh, Jim!
We have been looking for you!"

The teacher said, "Where have you been? Where are the other children?"

"I'll take you there," Jim said.

Jim started back.

He went past the penguins, past the deer.

This way? No! That way!

There they were—George, Willy and Sammy,

Anna Maria, Danny, Paul, and Sara.

When they saw their teacher,
George and Sara began to cry.
She hugged them.
"If we had stayed together, this
wouldn't have happened," she said.

Willy and Sammy said, "Jim was brave.
He went to find you!"

"Yes," the teacher said, "Jim was very brave.
But next time, remember—IF WE ALL STAY
TOGETHER, NOBODY WILL GET LOST."

They were so glad to be found!
Everybody went to have lunch in the cafeteria.
You could choose chicken and dumplings,
crisp fried fish, or beef stew with two vegetables.
But they all chose hot dogs.

Museum Map

Here is a map of the museum the first grade visited. Some children got lost. This map might have helped them. It shows the rooms in the museum.

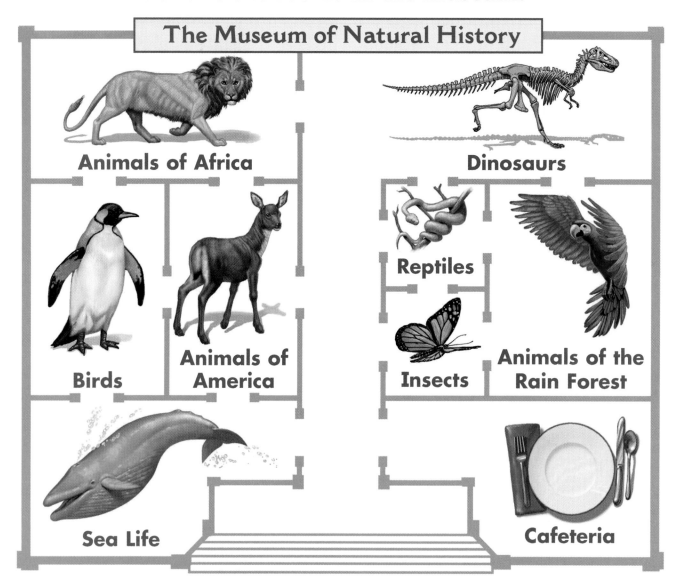

The Museum of Natural History

Animals of Africa

Dinosaurs

Birds

Animals of America

Reptiles

Insects

Animals of the Rain Forest

Sea Life

Cafeteria

Let's Talk

Where did Jim find his teacher?
What could you see in this museum?

About the Author and the Illustrator

Author

Miriam Cohen

Miriam Cohen wrote eighteen books about Jim and the other first graders. Ms. Cohen says that Jim is based on her three sons. She says Jim is a "rolling and patting together of Adam, Gabe, and Jem into one little guy."

Illustrator

Lillian Hoban

Do you like to visit museums? Lillian Hoban did when she was your age. Those visits may have given her ideas for the pictures in *Lost in the Museum.*

Ms. Hoban also loved to draw and read as a child. Now she draws the pictures for all of Miriam Cohen's books.

Let's Talk

What would you want to
see in the museum?
What would you do if
you got lost?

Readers Theater

Read and act out the story as a play.

1. One person reads what the teacher says.

2. Choose who will read the parts of Jim, Anna Maria,
   Sara, Danny, Paul, Willy, Sammy, and George.

3. Choose other children to play the rest of the
   first-grade class.

What Kind of Story?

Adjectives are words that describe. Some adjectives tell what kind.

Lost in the Museum is a **scary** story.

Name of Story	What Kind of Story
Arthur's Reading Race	funny
Lost!	good
Foal	true
Lost in the Museum	scary

Talk

What other stories have you read? Tell what kind of stories they are.

Write

Make a chart. Write names of books you have read. List adjectives that tell what kind of books they are.

Chompy's Afternoon

by G. Brian Karas

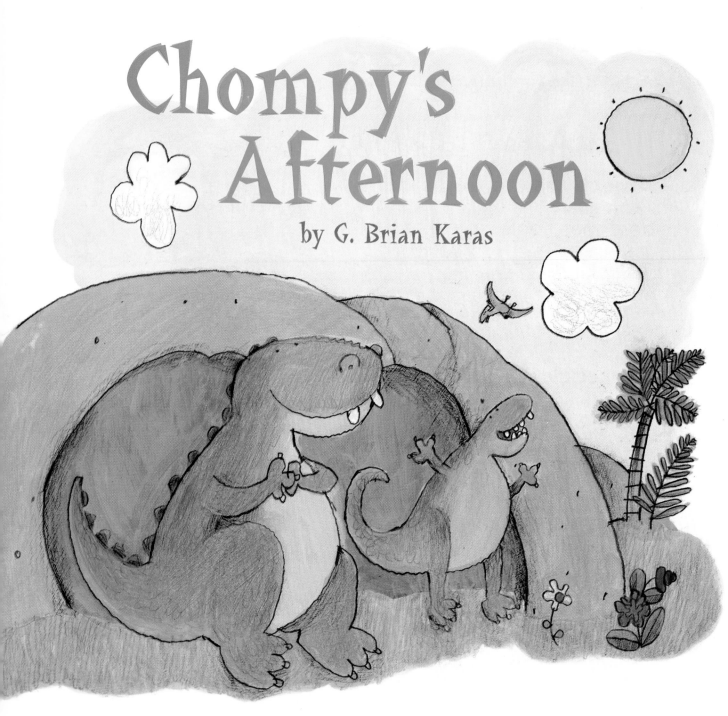

Chompy looked up at the blue sky.
"It's a nice afternoon," he said.
    "Let's have a picnic," said Mom.
    "I'm so happy!" said Chompy.
Chompy loved picnics more than
anything.

Chompy packed yummy food. He
packed everything he could find. "I'll
even pack these huge watermelons,"
he said.

Chompy was very hungry.

"My, my, Chompy. This is too much food," said Mom.

"I'll try to carry it," said Chompy. Chompy couldn't carry it all.

So Mom put most of the food back. Then she packed two cupcakes.

Chompy and his mom walked up
the pathway to a hilltop. They sat
down by a waterfall.
"It's very pretty here," said Mom.
They ate most of their food.

"I'm still hungry. I think I'll take a little walk," Chompy thought. Chompy looked around for more food.

"There has to be something to eat somewhere!" he thought.

"I'm so lucky," said Chompy.
"Here is a nice little treat." He took a
big bite.

But it was not nice or little or a
treat. It was a huge, mean animal.

Chompy heard a big roar.
"I'm not so lucky!" yelled Chompy.
He ran as fast as he could.
Mom heard Chompy cry. "Go
away, you big bully!" she roared.

The animal ran far away. Chompy
and his mom went back to the
hilltop.

"Here is a little treat, Chompy,"
said Mom. "And it won't bite back."
Chompy was very happy now.

Dinosaur Babies

by Lucille Recht Penner
illustrated by Peter Barrett

Apatosaurus
(a–PAT–uh–sor–us)

Squeak! Squeak!

Is that the sound of a baby

dinosaur calling to its mother?

Nobody knows.

Nobody has ever heard

a baby dinosaur.

Nobody has seen one.

All the dinosaurs died millions of years ago.
But we know a lot about them from what
dinosaur hunters have found . . .

footprints

teeth

bones

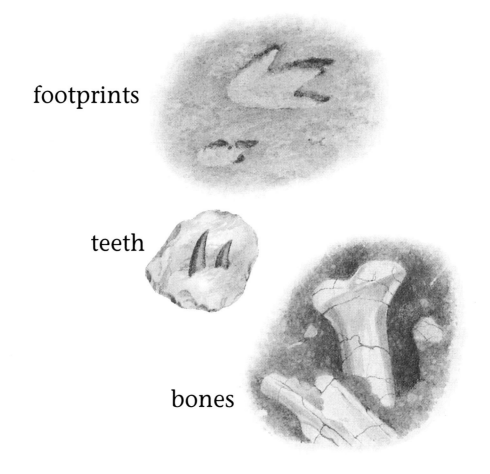

They have found small baby bones in nests.

They have even found dinosaur eggs.

Most dinosaurs were very big.

But their eggs were small.

The smallest was only as big as a quarter.

The biggest was about the size
of a football!

Were dinosaurs good mothers?

This kind of dinosaur was.

She made a nest of mud and

laid her eggs in it.

Chickens sit on their eggs.

But this dinosaur did not.

She was too heavy.

The eggs would break!

She put leaves on the eggs

to keep them warm.

Maiasaura
(my-uh-SOR-uh)

The mother watched the nest.

Lots of animals liked to eat dinosaur eggs!

She kept them away.

Inside the eggs the babies grew.
They breathed through tiny holes
in the eggshells.

One day the eggs
cracked!
Little baby dinosaurs
came out.
They were hungry.
Maybe they squeaked.

The mother dinosaur
brought them food.
The babies ate and ate
all day long.

Dinosaur babies had big heads and big eyes.

They could see and hear well.

Human babies are born without any teeth.

Not dinosaur babies! They had lots of teeth.

Tyrannosaurus
(tie-RAN-uh-SOR-us)

What did baby dinosaurs eat?
Some kinds ate leaves and
berries and seeds.

Some kinds ate little animals and bugs.

Deinonychus
(die–NON–ee–kus)

Was it safe for baby dinosaurs
to hunt for food alone? No!
Enemies were all around.
And baby dinosaurs could not
fight or run fast.
They could only hide.

Psittacosaurus
(SIT–uh–ko–SOR–us)

Triceratops
(try–SER–uh–tops)

Some baby dinosaurs were lucky.

They were never alone.

They lived in herds.

Even then enemies tried to grab
the babies and eat them!

So the dinosaurs made a circle.

Little ones stayed on the inside.

Big ones guarded the outside.

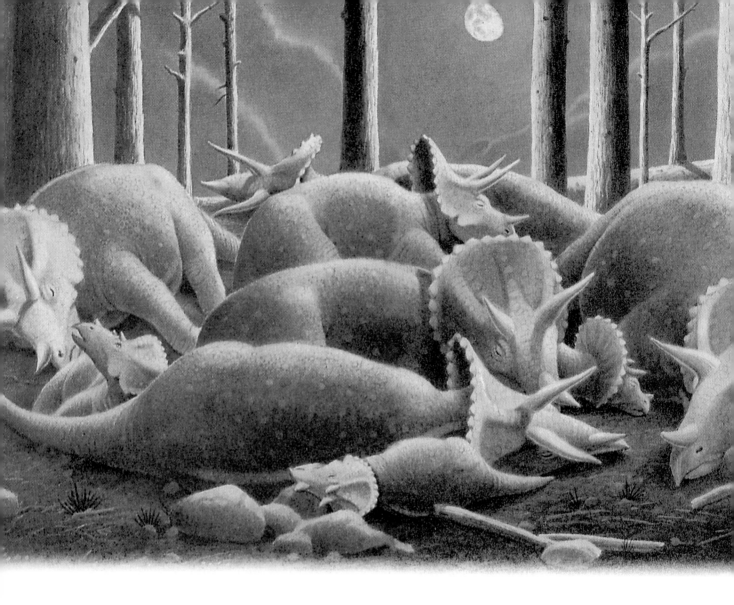

Babies were safe in the
dinosaur herd.
The dinosaurs walked and
ate and slept together.

Baby dinosaurs kept growing and changing.

Styracosaurus
(sty–RAK–uh–SOR–us)

Some kinds grew
sharp horns.

Some kinds grew
spikes on their tails.

Stegosaurus
(STEG–uh–SOR–us)

Others grew bony frills.

Protoceratops
(PRO–tuh–SER–uh–tops)

They grew until they weren't babies anymore.
Some grew to be the biggest animals ever to walk the Earth!
And some had dinosaur babies of their own.

Something Big Has Been Here

by Jack Prelutsky

Something big has been here,
what it was, I do not know,
for I did not see it coming,
and I did not see it go,
but I hope I never meet it,
if I do, I'm in a fix,
for it left behind its footprints,
they are size nine-fifty-six.

Unfortunately

by Bobbi Katz

Dinosaurs lived so long ago
they never had a chance to know
how many kids would love to get
a dinosaur to be their pet!

Let's Talk

What did you learn about dinosaurs?

What surprised you?

Make a Dinosaur

What you need:

clay

shoe box

rocks, pinecones, twigs

paper and art supplies

What you do:

Make a dinosaur out of clay.

Make a home for your dinosaur. Put it inside.

Write your dinosaur's name on top of the box.

How Many?

Words for numbers can be **adjectives**.
These adjectives tell how many.

This dinosaur has **three** horns.
There are **ten** eggs in the nest.

Talk

What do you know
about dinosaurs?
Tell a dinosaur fact.
Use an adjective that
tells how many.

Write

Write about dinosaurs.

The True Story of Abbie Burgess

by Fay Robinson
illustrated by Lane DuPont

Abbie Burgess watches her dad leave. While he is away, she'll do his job.

She'll light the lamps in the
lighthouse. The lamps help people
in boats see the rocks better.

Abbie looks out at the sea. She puts out her hand. She feels a few raindrops. The wind blows branches into the blue water and tosses the boats around. A big storm is on its way!

Abbie knows she must
light the lamps right away.
She dashes up the steps.
Rain washes over the
lighthouse.

Abbie lights the lamps one by one.
Now boat crews can see the rocks,
and they can keep their boats away.
   Abbie watches as a boat passes
by safely.

All night, Abbie rushes up
the steps to check the lights.
They must stay lit. She doesn't
sleep at all. She won't give up.
At last, the night is over.
Abbie's dad will be back soon.

But her dad can't come back because it is still raining!

Night after night, Abbie lights the lamps. Again and again, boats go around the rocks safely.

At last, the storm is over. Abbie's
dad comes back. He gives Abbie a hug.
He knew she could do the job!
Abbie Burgess helped a lot of people.
She was a true hero.

The Bravest Cat!
The True Story of Scarlett

by Laura Driscoll

illustrated by Fred Willingham

Brooklyn, NY, 1996

A building is on fire!

There are lots of fire engines and
lots of firemen.

It is a big fire in an old garage.

But one thing is lucky.

No one lives in the building.

Wait! Look!

What do the firemen see?

It is a cat!

She runs out of the garage.

She is carrying something—

something small.

It is a tiny kitten!

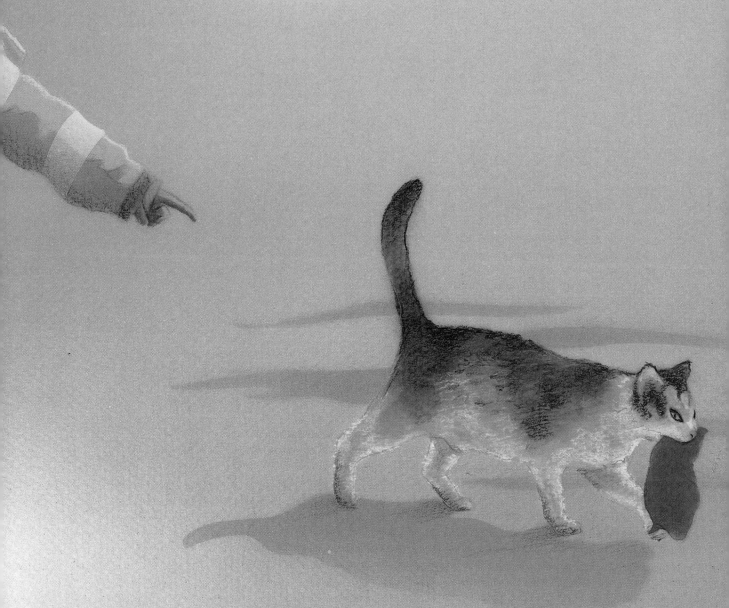

The cat puts her kitten
in a safe place.
Then she runs back into the fire!
What is she doing?

Soon the cat runs out again—
with another kitten!

She runs in and out

three more times.

The firemen cannot believe their eyes.

Now there is a pile of kittens!

They are tiny and scared.

One has burns on his little ears.

And the poor mother cat!

Her burns are bad.

Her eyes are hurt.

She cannot even see her kittens.

So she touches each kitten with
her nose.

One, two, three, four, five.

They are all there.

Very gently, a fireman puts
all of the cats into a box.
He can tell they need a doctor.
The fireman takes the cats to
the animal hospital.

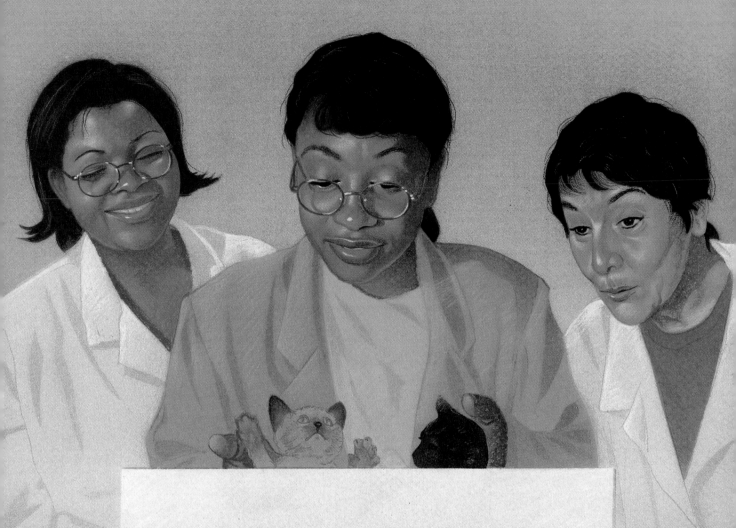

The cats do not belong to anyone.
They are strays. So the doctors
give the mother cat a name.
They call her Scarlett because of
her red burns.

Soon lots of people
know about Scarlett.
Newspapers run stories.
People want her to be on TV.
She is a hero and a star.

Everyone hopes Scarlett will get better.
And slowly she does.
The kittens are kept in another room
so she can rest.
Scarlett cannot take care of
them anymore.

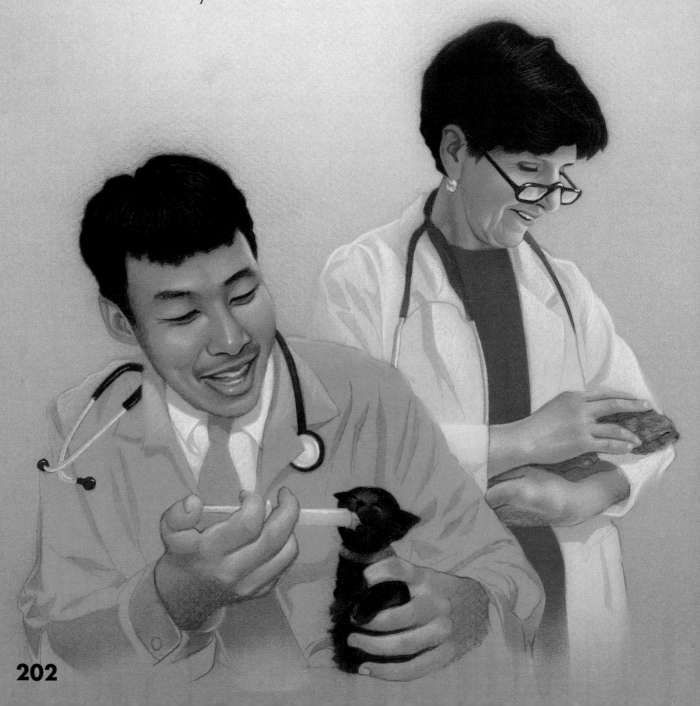

The people at the hospital
give the kittens lots of love.
And they get better too—
all except one.
The doctors think he was the last
kitten to get out of the fire.
The smoke hurt his lungs.
A month later, he dies.

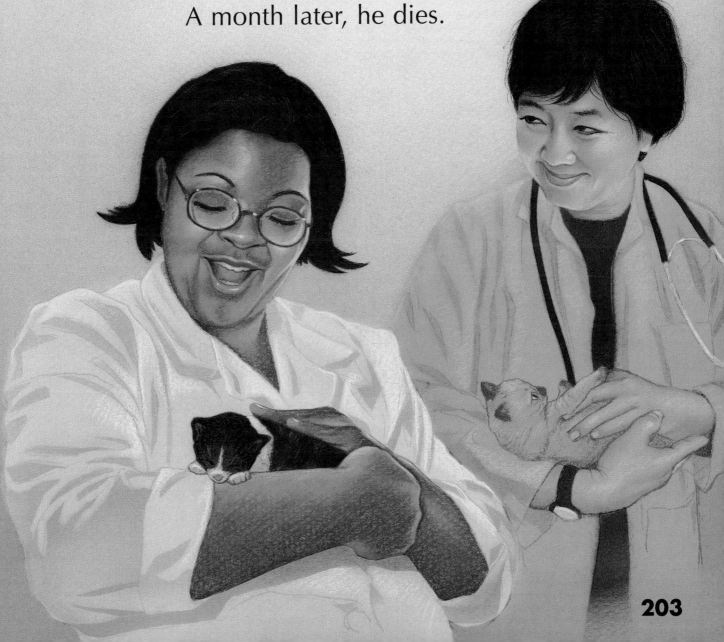

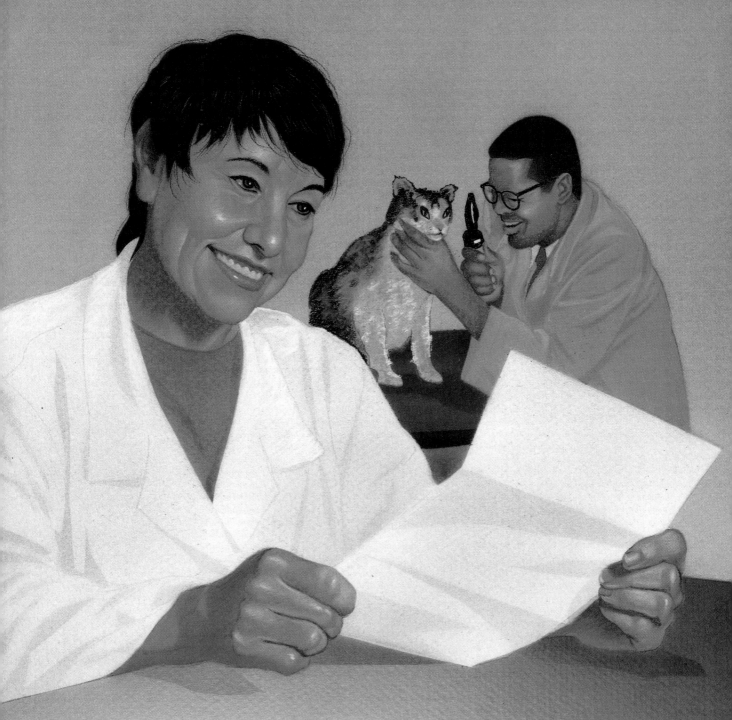

But the other kittens get new homes.
And what about Scarlett?
Letters for her come from all
over the world.
So many people want to give her
a good home.

The people at the hospital
read more than 1,000 letters!
They try to find the best home
for Scarlett.

At last, they make up their minds.
TV and newspaper reporters
come to hear the big news.
A woman named Karen Wellen
will care for Scarlett.

In her letter, Karen wrote
about her own accident—
a car accident.
Like Scarlett, it took a long time
for Karen to get better.
She knows what Scarlett
has been through.

Karen also had a cat before.

She loved it a lot.

But Karen's cat died just after
her accident.

Karen did not want to get another cat—
unless it was a very special one . . .

just like Scarlett!

About the Illustrator

Fred Willingham

To make his drawings look
real, Fred Willingham looks at photographs
as he draws. Sometimes he takes the photographs.
He uses his children and his friends as models.
He used photos of cats in many poses when he
drew the pictures for *The Bravest Cat!* He found
those photos at the library. He knew just how to
draw Scarlett because he saw a photograph of her.

Kittens

by Myra Cohn Livingston

Our cat had kittens
weeks ago
when everything outside was snow.

So she stayed in
and kept them warm
and safe from all the clouds and storm.

But yesterday
when there was sun
she snuzzled on the smallest one

and turned it over
from beneath
and took its fur between her teeth

and carried it
outside to see
how nice a winter day can be

and then our dog
decided he
would help her take the other three

and one by one
they took them out
to see what sun is all about

so when they're grown
they'll always know
to never be afraid of snow.

Reader Response

Let's Talk

Scarlett was a hero.

Who do you think is a hero?

What did that hero do?

Make an Award for Your Hero

What you need:

colored paper

crayon or markers

art supplies

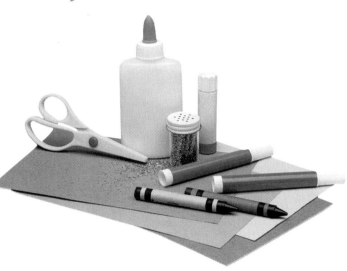

What you do:

Cut out parts of the award.

Glue them together.

Write the name of your hero.

214

An Animal I Know

An **adjective** tells more about a person, place, animal, or thing. Adjectives make sentences better.

My dad has a **special** dog. Drew has **black** fur and a **long** tail. He keeps Dad safe when they walk. Drew is Dad's **good** friend.

Talk

Describe an animal. Tell about its color, size, and shape. How else can you describe it?

Write

Write about an animal. Use adjectives.

Glossary

Words from Your Stories

Aa

accident   An **accident** is something bad that happens. We were in a car **accident**.

across   He rode the bicycle **across** the tightrope.

across

almost   I **almost** missed the bus. It is **almost** ten o'clock.

Bb

baby   A **baby** is a very young child or animal. A **baby** cat is called a kitten.

believe   When you **believe** something, you think it is true.

beneath   **Beneath** means below or under. The dog's bone is **beneath** the bed.

beneath

bought   He **bought** a new pair of shoes.

break   If you **break** something, it comes apart or goes to pieces.

breathed   If you **breathed**, you took in air through your nose or mouth.

buildings Buildings have walls and a roof. Schools and houses are **buildings**.

building

burns **Burns** are sores caused by too much heat. He got **burns** from the hot pan.

Cc

cafeteria A **cafeteria** is a place to eat in a school or other building. You choose your food and carry it to a table.

climbed If you **climbed**, you went up something. The squirrels **climbed** the post.

could Her brother said she **could** come. She **could** run very fast.

crowded **Crowded** means too full. The bus was very **crowded** this morning.

climbed

crowded

crying If you are **crying**, you have tears coming from your eyes.

curb A **curb** is the raised edge between the sidewalk and street.

217

Dd

dinosaur A **dinosaur** is an animal that lived many years ago. **Dinosaurs** lived on Earth before there were people.

disappears When something **disappears**, it goes out of sight.

Ee

Earth **Earth** is the planet we live on.

eight **Eight** is one more than seven, 8. Can you count **eight** cats?

else Will someone **else** go in my place? Let's go somewhere **else** for lunch.

enemies Your **enemies** are people or animals that wish to harm you.

eight

except The store is open every day **except** Sunday.

Ff

field A **field** is a piece of land without trees. The cows grazed in the **field.**

field

fierce **Fierce** means very strong or dangerous.

fooling If you are **fooling**, you are joking, teasing, or pretending.

found She **found** a hat in the hall. She took it to the Lost and **Found**.

fur **Fur** is hair that is thick and soft. **Fur** covers the skin of many animals.

Gg

garage A **garage** is a place where cars are parked.

garage

guarded If you **guarded** something, you kept it safe. The dog **guarded** the house.

Hh

happened When something has **happened**, it has taken place.

heavy When something is **heavy**, it weighs very much. A piano is **heavy**.

heavy

herds **Herds** are groups of animals that live, move, and feed together.

hero A **hero** is someone admired for his or her bravery or good deeds.

hooves

hooves **Hooves** are more than one **hoof**. Horses, cows, and pigs have **hooves**.

hospital   A **hospital** is a place where sick people are cared for.

human   A **human** body is the body of a person.

hunters   **Hunters** are people who kill wild birds or animals for food or for sport.

hurried   If you **hurried**, you went very quickly. He **hurried** to catch the school bus.

hurried

hurt   If you **hurt** something or someone, you cause it pain.

Kk

knew   I **knew** her name. He **knew** the answer.

Ll

library   A **library** is a room or building where books are kept. You can take books out at most **libraries**.

library

Mm

millions   **Millions** means more than one million. A **million** is one thousand thousand, or 1,000,000.

minds When people make up their **minds**, they decide about something.

months **Months** are parts of a year. There are twelve **months** in a year.

months

museum A **museum** is a building for keeping and showing interesting things.

Nn

neigh To **neigh** is to make the sound that a horse makes.

newborn **Newborn** means only just born.

noisy **Noisy** means full of noise. It is very **noisy** near the airport.

Oo

opened When something has been **opened**, people and things can get in or out of it. The cat **opened** the drawer.

opened

otter An **otter** is an animal with thick brown fur and strong claws.

Pp

paint   **Paint** is a liquid used to color things. **Paint** comes in many different colors.

penguins   **Penguins** are sea birds that dive and swim but do not fly. **Penguins** live in very cold places.

people   Men, women, and children are **people.**

ponies   **Ponies** are small horses.

prove   To **prove** something is to show that it is true.

penguins

Rr

reporters   **Reporter**s are people who write or tell news for a newspaper, magazine, or a radio or TV station.

roar   A **roar** is a loud, deep sound. The lion's **roar** frightened us.

Ss

safely   **Safely** means without harm or danger.

scared   **Scared** means afraid.

shook   If you **shook** your head, you moved it from side to side. It is a way to say no.

signs

signs   **Signs** are marks or words used to tell you something. Cars stop at stop **signs.**

222

soft Soft means not loud.

special Something that is **special** is unusual or different.

spy When you **spy** something, you see it and notice it. Meg **spies** footprints.

spy

stronger If you feel **stronger**, you have more power and health than before.

struggle To **struggle** is to work at something that is hard to do. Each team **struggled** to win.

struggle

Tt

thought If you had an idea about something, then you **thought** about it.

through The bird flew **through** the house. Are you **through** with your dinner?

Ww

wobbly Wobbly means shaky.

worry To **worry** is to feel upset and afraid.

Tested Word List

A Real Gift
Arthur's Reading Race

buy
only
or
right
think

A Big Day for Jay
Lost!

don't
from
hear
live
when

Baby Otter Grows Up
Foal

around
her
new
old
show

What a Sight!
Lost in the Museum

been
first
found
start
together

Chompy's Afternoon
Dinosaur Babies

animals
even
heard
most
their

The True Story of Abbie Burgess
The Bravest Cat! The True Story of Scarlett

because
better
burns
give
people
put

Acknowledgments

Text

Page 18: *Arthur's Reading Race* by Marc Brown, pp. 2–23. Text and illustrations copyright © 1996 by Marc Brown. Reprinted by permission of Random House, Inc.
Page 52: *Lost!* by David McPhail. Copyright © 1990 by David McPhail. Reprinted by permission of Little, Brown and Company.
Page 90: *Foal* by Mary Ling, photographed by Gordon Clayton, pp. 6–21. Copyright © 1992 by Dorling Kindersley Limited, London. Reprinted by permission of Dorling Kindersley Publishing, Inc.
Page 106: "Everything Grows" words by Raffi, D. Pike, music by Raffi. Copyright © 1987 by Homeland Publishing (CAPAC), a division of Troubadour Records Ltd. All rights reserved. Reprinted by permission of Troubadour Records Ltd.
Page 118: *Lost in the Museum* by Miriam Cohen, pictures by Lillian Hoban. Text copyright © 1979 by Miriam Cohen. Illustrations copyright © 1979 by Lillian Hoban. Reprinted by permission of Greenwillow Books, a division of William Morrow & Company, Inc.
Page 156: *Dinosaur Babies* by Lucille Recht Penner, illustrated by Peter Barrett. Text copyright © 1991 by Lucille Recht Penner. Illustrations copyright © 1991 by Peter Barrett. Reprinted by permission of Random House, Inc.
Page 178: "Something Big Has Been Here" from *Something Big Has Been Here* poems by Jack Prelutsky, p. 7. Text copyright © 1990 by Jack Prelutsky. Reprinted by permission of Greenwillow Books, a division of William Morrow & Company, Inc.

Page 179: "Unfortunately" by Bobbi Katz. Copyright © 1976, renewed © 1995 by Bobbi Katz. Reprinted by permission of the poet.
Page 190: Abridgment of *The Bravest Cat!* by Laura Driscoll. Text copyright © 1997 by Laura Driscoll. Reprinted by permission of Grosset & Dunlap, Inc., a division of Penguin Putnam, Inc.
Page 212: "Kittens" from *Worlds I Know and Other Poems* by Myra Cohn Livingston. Text copyright © 1985 by Myra Cohn Livingston. Reprinted by permission of Margaret K. McElderry Books, an imprint of Simon & Schuster Children's Publishing Division.

Artists

Maryjane Begin, cover, 8–9
Marc Brown, 18–41
Benton Mahan, 42
Lily Hong Hatch, 44–51
David McPhail, 52–79
Rusty Fletcher, 80–81
Anna Vojtech, 82–88
Jack Wallen, 106
Kate Flanagan, 109
Darryl Ligasan, 110–117
Lillian Hoban, 118–143
Walter Stuart, 144
Jerry Tiritilli, 146–147
G. Brian Karas, 148–155
Peter Barrett, 156–177
Claudia Sargent, (border) 156
Allan Eitzen, 178, 179
Randy Chewning, 180–181

Lane DuPont, 182–189
Fred Willingham, 190–209
Stephanie Britt, 212–213
Anthony Carnabuci, 214–215

Photographs

Page 5 Richard Hutchings for Scott Foresman
Pages 10–17 Lawrence Migdale for Scott Foresman
Page 41 Courtesy Marc Brown
Page 79 Richard Hutchings for Scott Foresman
Page 82 Alan D. Carey/Photo Researchers
Page 89 Walter Chandoha
Pages 90–105 Gordon Clayton
Pages 106, 107 Bruce McMillan
Page 145 (T) Courtesy Miriam Cohen; (B) Courtesy William Morrow
Page 210 Chris Kasson/AP/Wide World
Page 211 Brent Jones for Scott Foresman

Glossary

The contents of this glossary have been adapted from *My First Picture Dictionary*, Revised Edition, Copyright © 1990 by Scott, Foresman and Company, or from *My Second Picture Dictionary*, Revised Edition, Copyright © 1990 by Scott, Foresman and Company.